One-Pan Meals

30 Cast-Iron Skillet Recipes with Fresh and Low-Carb Ingredients Perfect for Your Healthy Holidays

Table of Contents

Author's Foreword

"No one is born a great cook; one learns by doing."

My mother once told me that cooking is a labor of love. I say that is true. Because whenever you spend time in the kitchen preparing and cooking meals for your family, you are showing them how much you love and appreciate them. That is why I grew up in the kitchen. I grew up watching my grandma and mom cook their way through every meal, every holiday and every joyous occasion.

I remember seeing my grandmother cooking delicious comfort food in her cast iron skillet. One which she hardly washes and hardly puts away. And I thought to myself, what makes the food from this pan come out great and comforting each and every time? Is it just the pan or is it also from the love and compassion that goes with every dish they make in it?

Our family's home cooked meals and my love for cooking new dishes in a cast iron skillet inspired me to create this book.

One-Pan Meals: 30 Cast-Iron Skillet Recipes with Fresh and Low-Carb Ingredients Perfect

for Your Healthy Holidays is a glimpse of how our love for food developed. Inside you will find:

- 30 amazingly delicious recipes that you can make using a cast iron pan. Each category has a specific chapter containing either: breakfast, dinner or dessert recipes made simple and healthier.

- All the nutrition information that you need per recipe. This will make sure that it meets the average 2,000 calorie intake of a person, or even those who are following a 1,200 calorie intake on a daily basis.

- Additional cooking suggestions, alternatives and tips that you can use when making these dishes.

- The advantages of using a cast iron skillet in your cooking.

- Plus, so much more!

Thank you for downloading this book and we are hoping that we can share our family's love for food through the recipes featured here.

9

Bonus: Your FREE Gift

As a token of our appreciation, please take advantage of the **FREE Gift** - a lifetime **VIP Membership** at our book club.

Follow the link below to download your FREE books:

http://bit.ly/vipbookclub

As a VIP member, you will get an instant **FREE** access to exclusive new releases and bestselling books.

"I think careful cooking is love, don't you? The loveliest thing you can cook for someone who's close to you is about as nice a valentine as you can give." – Julia Child

Chapter One: 10 Healthy One-Pan Holiday Breakfasts

Breakfast is a meal that I can and will never take for granted. As a matter of fact, I plan my breakfast more than the other meals during the day. And because I am a busy mother of 2 growing children, I always make sure that I have our first meal of the day ready on time without the fuss of washing and cleaning up.

In this chapter, I will help you:

- Learn new ways to make healthy breakfasts using a single pan or skillet.

- Find out different tips and suggestions on how to make your cooking experience easier.

Holiday Meal Planning: 10 Healthy Holiday Breakfasts using a Cast Iron Skillet

The following are easy and really tasty breakfast recipes that can be made using a single skillet. These recipes are perfect for any type of holidays or during days that you just want to serve something fancy and delicious.

Florentine Hash Skillet

What You Need:

- 1 tsp of extra virgin olive oil
- ½ cup of frozen or fresh hash browns
- 1 large organic egg
- ½ cup of frozen, thawed spinach
- 2 tbsp. of grated sharp cheddar cheese
- A pinch of salt and pepper

Let's Make It:

1. Heat oil in your skillet over medium to high heat.
2. Add the hash browns and spread it evenly. Add a layer of frozen spinach and crack an egg in the middle. Season with salt and pepper.

3. Cover the pan and reduce the heat to low and cook until the eggs are set but the yolks are still runny. This should take about 7 to 10 minutes.

Nutritional Information

- Vegetarian, Healthy Aging, Low Carb, Low calorie, High in Calcium, High in Protein

Prep Time:	5 minutes
Cook Time:	10 minutes
Total Time:	15 minutes
Servings	1 to 2
Calories	226
Total Fat	15 grams
Saturated Fat	5 grams
Protein	14 grams
Cholesterol	200 mg
Carbohydrates	11 grams

Extra Tip:

- You can use a package of pre-cooked shredded potatoes to really cut your time in half.

- If you are using a bigger cast iron skillet, you can crack up to 4 eggs in there for more servings.

Savory Bread Pudding with Mushrooms

What You Need:

- 4 large organic eggs
- 2 cups of milk (low fat)
- ½ tsp of hot sauce
- ¾ tsp of salt, divided
- 1 (10 oz.) package of frozen spinach, thawed
- 3 and ½ cups of day-old bread, cut into cubes
- 1 Tbsp. of extra virgin olive oil
- 1 cup chopped yellow onions
- 1 (12 oz.) pack of button mushrooms sliced
- 1 large clove of garlic, crushed
- 1 cup of grated gruyere or manchego cheese

Let's Make It:

1. Preheat your oven to 350 degrees F. and heat up the oil in a skillet.

2. Start by sautéing the garlic, onions, and sliced mushrooms until browned. Add spinach and season well with salt and pepper. Set aside to cool. Do not wash the cast iron skillet because you will be using it after.

3. In a bowl, combine the eggs, milk, tabasco and salt. Mix well and add the cheese. Once the mushroom mixture is cool enough, add it to your egg mixture and mix well.

4. Lastly, add the cubed bread and transfer the mixture in your cast iron skillet.

5. Bake for about 50 to 60 minutes or until the eggs are set and the edges have browned.

Nutritional Information

- Vegetarian/ Vegan-friendly, Low Calorie, High Protein

Prep Time:	30 minutes
Cook Time:	1 hour
Total Time:	1 hour and 30 minutes

Servings	6
Calories	282
Total Fat	14 grams
Saturated Fat	6 grams
Protein	18 grams
Cholesterol	148 mg
Carbohydrates	23 grams

One Skillet Shakshuka

What You Need:

- 6 organic eggs
- 1 (28 oz.) jar of organic tomato sauce
- 1 tsp. of cumin
- 1/4 tsp of red pepper flakes
- 5 large cloves garlic, minced
- 1 yellow or red onion, chopped
- 1 red bell pepper, sliced into thin strips
- 1 tbsp. of chopped parsley
- 1/4 tsp of iodized salt
- 1/2 tsp of freshly ground black pepper
- 1 (1.6 oz.) pack of feta cheese, cubed or crumbled
- parsley, for garnish
- water or olive oil for sautéing

Let's Make It:

1. Heat up your cast iron skillet, heat up about a tablespoon of water or oil. Sauté garlic, onions, and bell pepper until fragrant and translucent.

2. Add the cumin, red pepper flakes, salt, and pepper to season. Then add the tomato sauce and mix well. Allow to boil for a few minutes or until the sauce has slightly thickened. Add the chopped parsley and mix again.

3. Crack the eggs on top of the sauce and add crumbled feta all over the skillet. Cook the eggs for 10 minutes or until the whites have set and the yolks are still runny.

4. Garnish with more parsley and feta.

Nutritional Information

- Low fat, vegetarian, high protein

Prep Time:	10 minutes
Cook Time:	30 minutes
Total Time:	40 minutes
Servings	6
Calories	272
Total Fat	10 grams
Saturated Fat	2 grams
Protein	12.2 grams

Cholesterol	186 mg
Carbohydrates	37 grams

Extra Tip:

- Do not reheat the eggs once they are cooked. Doing so will leave you with really rubbery eggs. If you want your dish to stay warm, cook the eggs minutes before you serve them.

Salmon Rostis

What You Need:

For the Rostis

- 2 (6 or 7 oz.) cans of boneless and skinless Alaskan salmon, drained
- ½ cup of red onions, finely chopped
- 2 large whole eggs+1 egg white, beaten
- 1 tbsp. of whole grain mustard
- ½ tsp of ground black pepper
- 3 tbsp. of chopped fresh dill
- ¼ tsp of salt
- 2 tbsp. of extra virgin olive oil
- 4 cups of frozen or pre-cooked hash browns or shredded potatoes

For the Sauce

- 1/3 cup of zero fat sour cream

- 1 tsp of fresh lemon juice
- 1 tbsp. of chopped capers

Let's Make It:

1. In a large bowl, combine the ingredients for the rosti except for the oil and the eggs. Make sure that you combine everything well before you add the eggs.
2. Form the mixture into patties and heat up your cast iron pan over medium heat.
3. Fry up the patties in olive oil and drain the excess fat on paper towels.
4. In a small bowl, combine the ingredients for the sauce and place in the fridge until you are ready to serve.

Nutritional Information

- Pescetarian, Low-Carb, Low-Added Sugar, Low-Calorie, Gluten Free

Prep Time:	10 minutes
Cook Time:	15 minutes
Total Time:	25 minutes
Servings	4 to 5
Calories	218

Total Fat	15 grams
Saturated Fat	3 grams
Protein	21 grams
Cholesterol	125 mg
Carbohydrates	15 grams

Baked Avocado and Eggs with Spicy Tomato Sauce

What You Need:

- 1 (10 oz.) can of Southern style diced tomatoes, slightly drained
- 1 ripe avocado, peeled and sliced into thin wedges
- 4 large eggs
- Salt, pepper, red pepper flakes to taste

Let's Make It:

1. In a cast iron skillet, heat up the tomatoes and season with salt, pepper and red pepper flakes. Cook the tomatoes down, about 6 minutes.
2. Arrange the avocado slices all around the skillet and crack an egg on top.
3. Cover and cook for 10 to 12 minutes. The egg whites should be set and but do not overcook.

Nutritional Information

- Low Carb, Vegetarian, Paleo friendly

Prep Time:	10 minutes
Cook Time:	20 minutes
Total Time:	30 minutes
Servings	4
Calories	224
Total Fat	19.1 grams
Saturated Fat	3.5 grams
Protein	7.6 grams
Cholesterol	156 mg
Carbohydrates	8.9 grams

Ground Turkey and Sweet Potato Skillet

What You Need:

- 2 tbsp. of extra-virgin olive oil
- 1 lb. of ground turkey, extra lean
- 1 large garlic clove, minced
- ½ cup of red onions, diced
- ½ cup of yellow pepper, diced
- 1 and ½ cups of sweet potato, diced
- Salt and pepper to taste
- A pinch of red chili flakes (more or less)
- ½ cup of shredded mozzarella cheese

Let's Make It:

1. In a large cast iron skillet, heat up some oil and sauté the onions, garlic, and the rest of the vegetables.

2. Cook until the sweet potatoes are tender. Season with salt, pepper and chili flakes.

3. While sweet potatoes are cooking, preheat the oven to 400 degrees F.

4. Once tender, turn the flame off and sprinkle the shredded mozzarella on top. Bake for 3 minutes or until the cheese has melted.

Nutritional Information

- Gluten Free, Low Carb, High Protein

Prep Time:	15 minutes
Cook Time:	15 minutes
Total Time:	30 minutes
Servings	4-6
Calories	245
Total Fat	13 grams
Saturated Fat	4.5 grams
Protein	19.83
Cholesterol	66 mg
Carbohydrates	10.38 grams

Extra Tip:

- I like my skillet extra spicy so you can serve this with more tabasco or any chili sauce you like.

Mushroom and Wild Rice Frittatas

What You Need:

For the Wild Rice

- ½ cup of wild rice – easy cook
- 2 cups of water
- Salt to taste

For the Frittata

- 5 large eggs
- 2 large egg whites
- 2 tbsp. chopped fresh parsley
- 1/2 tsp salt, divided
- 1 cup chopped red onion
- 1 tbsp. minced fresh rosemary or 1 tsp of dried herb
- 1 pound sliced mixed mushrooms (cremini, white button, shiitake)

- 1/2 cup shredded Parmesan cheese
- 4 slices of chopped prosciutto (about 2 ounces)
- 2 tsp. extra virgin olive oil
- ¼ tsp nutmeg
- ½ tsp of pepper, divided

Let's Make It:

1. First cook the rice in your skillet according to package directions. Once cooked, transfer to a separate container and set aside.

2. In a bowl, combine the eggs, half the salt, half the pepper and nutmeg. Add the parsley. Set aside.

3. Take your skillet and heat up some oil. Sauté the onions, prosciutto and rice. Once browned, add the mushrooms and the seasonings.

4. Slowly stir in the eggs to make sure that everything ingredient is evenly distributed. Cover and cook on low flame for 30 minutes or until the eggs are fully cooked.

Nutritional Information

- Low calorie, Low Carb, Low Sugar, Gluten Free, Low fat

Prep Time:	15 minutes
Cook Time:	45 minutes
Total Time:	1 hour
Servings	6
Calories	210
Total Fat	9 grams
Saturated Fat	3 grams
Protein	16 grams
Cholesterol	168 mg
Carbohydrates	18 grams

Extra Tip:

- If you cannot find instant cook wild rice, you can pre-cook the rice ahead of time.

Egg and Sausage Breakfast Casserole

What You Need:

- 1 (5 oz.) package of turkey breakfast sausage, casing removed
- 1 tsp of canola oil
- 1 yellow onion, chopped
- 1 medium red bell pepper, chopped
- 4 large organic eggs,
- 4 large egg whites
- 2 and ½ cups of low-fat fresh milk
- 1 tsp of dry mustard
- ¼ tsp of black pepper
- ½ tsp of salt
- 2/3 cup of grated sharp cheddar cheese, divided

- 10 slices of white or whole wheat bread, remove the crusts

Let's Make It:

1. Cook your sausages in a skillet until completely browned. Sauté the onions and bell peppers until fragrant and soft. Remove from the pan and set aside.

2. Layer the bread in a large skillet. Set aside.

3. In a large bowl, combine the eggs, milk, dry mustard, salt, pepper and half of the cheese. Mix until well combined.

4. Pour the egg mixture over the bread layer and then top with the cooked sausages and veggies. Spread evenly and cover with foil or a sheet of saran wrap. Place in the fridge and allow to marinate for 5 hours or more.

5. Once you are ready to bake, preheat your oven to 350 degrees F.

6. Sprinkle the remaining cheese on top and bake for 30 to 40 minutes or until the eggs are cooked and the tops have browned.

Nutritional Information

- Low Calorie, Low Carb, Low Sodium

Prep Time:	6 hours
Cook Time:	40 minutes
Total Time:	6 hours and 40 minutes
Servings	12
Calories	141
Total Fat	7 grams
Saturated Fat	3 grams
Protein	10 grams
Cholesterol	90 mg
Carbohydrates	10 grams

Extra Tip:

- This is a great make-ahead holiday breakfast, so do not hesitate to make large batches if you want to serve this to your entire family.

Spinach, Eggs and Mushrooms

What You Need:

- 1 tbsp., of extra virgin olive oil (for cooking the mushrooms)
- 1 (8 oz.) pack of mini-Bella mushrooms, chopped
- 1 (10 oz.) pack of fresh spinach or about 5-6 cups of firmly packed fresh spinach
- 3-4 large eggs
- Salt and Pepper, to season

Let's Make It:

1. In a large cast iron skillet, heat the oil and sauté the mushrooms until brown and soft. Add the spinach and season with salt and pepper. Once the spinach has wilted, spread the mixture evenly.
2. Crack 3 to 4 eggs on top and cover to cook. The eggs should be set and the yolk should be runny. This can take up to 7 to 8 minutes depending on the size of the eggs.

Nutritional Information

Prep Time:	5 minutes

Cook Time:	15 minutes
Total Time:	20 minutes
Servings	4
Calories	137
Total Fat	6.8 grams
Saturated Fat	2 grams
Protein	14.7 grams
Cholesterol	196 mg
Carbohydrates	5 grams

Polenta Breakfast Skillet with Eggs

What You Need:

- 3/4 cup of cornmeal or instant dry polenta
- 2 and ½ cups of vegetable stock
- 1 cup of grated cheddar cheese
- ¼ cup of chopped cilantro
- Salt and pepper to taste
- 6 large eggs

Let's Make It:

1. In a large cast iron skillet, bring the stock to a simmer and add the polenta. Continue mixing until thick and creamy.
2. Season with salt, pepper and cheese. Mix well.
3. Crack the eggs on top and cover for 5 more minutes or until the eggs are cooked. Add more cheese and chopped cilantro before serving.

Nutritional Information

- Low sodium, low-calorie, low-carb, vegetarian, low-fat

Prep Time:	15 minutes
Cook Time:	10 minutes
Total Time:	25 minutes
Servings	6
Calories	204
Total Fat	7.5 grams
Saturated Fat	2.6 grams
Protein	10.7 grams
Cholesterol	190 mg
Carbohydrates	24 grams

"Fall in love with taking care of yourself. Mind. Body. Spirit."

Chapter Two: 10 Healthy Cast-Iron Pan Holiday Dinner Recipes

It is always great to come home to a delicious holiday dinner. At the same time, it would also be amazing if you would be able to pull off a really gorgeous spread despite your busy schedule. The following recipes will surely help you make that happen.

In this chapter, I will help you:

- Cook one-pan recipes that are not just perfect for the holidays but also perfect for those who are living healthier lifestyles.

- Understand that cooking should not be complicated to be appetizing and tasty at the same time.

Healthy Holiday Dinners Using One Cast Iron Skillet

Are you ready to make healthy dishes worthy of the holidays? The following one-pan recipes will surely be the perfect ones to try.

Basque Vegetable Rice

What You Need:

- 2 tbsp. of extra virgin olive oil
- 1 medium-sized onion, chopped
- 1 small dried (red) Chile pepper, crushed
- 2 large cloves of garlic, minced
- 2 large ripe Roma tomatoes, seeded and chopped
- 1 red bell pepper, diced
- 1 medium zucchini, chopped
- 1 tsp of the following:
  - Dried thyme
  - Spanish paprika

- ½ tsp of fine salt
- A pinch of black pepper
- 3 cups of vegetable broth (low-sodium)
- 1 and ¼ cups of short grain white rice
- 2 tbsp. of freshly chopped parsley
- 6 slices of lemon

Let's Make It:

1. In your large 12-inch cast iron pan or skillet, heat the oil and start sautéing the onions, garlic, chili pepper and bell pepper until soft and fragrant. Do not burn the garlic or the entire dish will taste bitter.

2. Add the diced tomatoes, cubed zucchini, paprika, salt, pepper, and thyme. Mix well and allow to simmer. Stir occasionally and cook for 15 minutes.

3. Add the rice and mix well. The tomato mixture should coat the rice grains. Add the broth and stir again. Cook for 20 to 30 minutes or until the rice grains are completely cooked and almost all the broth has been absorbed.

4. Garnish with parsley and lemon wedges.

Nutritional Information

- Low Fat, Vegetarian, Gluten Free, Vegan-Friendly, Low Carb, Zero Cholesterol

Prep Time:	30 minutes
Cook Time:	1 hour and 10 minutes
Total Time:	1 hour and 40 minutes
Servings	6
Calories	206
Total Fat	5 grams
Saturated Fat	1 gram
Protein	4 grams
Cholesterol	0 mg
Carbohydrates	35 grams

Extra Tip:

- While any good quality short grain rice will work, I usually go for the "paella" kind of rice grains such as Valencia.

Stuffed Heritage Pork Chops

What You Need:

For the Pork:

- 4 cups of water
- 4 cups of fresh orange juice
- 2 pieces of jalapeno peppers, roughly chopped
- 1/4 cup of tightly packed brown sugar
- 2 and 1/2 tbsps. of fine sea salt
- 4 (8 oz.) center cut heritage pork chops, bone in
- 2 rashers of bacon, chopped
- 1/2 cup of finely diced yellow onion
- 1/4 cup of finely diced apple
- 1/4 cup of mushrooms, sliced
- 1/4 cup of finely cubed butternut squash
- 1/4 cup of finely chopped Swiss chard

- 1 large garlic clove, minced
- 1/4 tsp each of salt and ground black pepper
- 1 tbsp. of extra virgin olive oil

For the Sauce:

- 1 and 1/2 cups of finely chopped onion
- 1/4 cup of finely chopped celery
- 1 tsp of minced jalapeño pepper
- 1 large garlic clove, minced
- 2 tbsp. of all-purpose flour
- 1/2 cup of beef broth – low-fat and low-sodium
- 1/2 cup of water
- 1/2 cup of unsalted canned tomatoes, chopped

Let's Make It:

1. In a large airtight container, combine water, orange juice, jalapeno peppers, salt, and brown sugar. Mix well and marinate the pork in the mixture. You can

do this at least 4 hours before you cook this. You can also make this the night before.

2. In order to make your filling, crisp up the bacon bits. Remove the cooked bacon and set aside. You can also drain some of the excess oil. Add the onions, diced apples, mushrooms, chopped butternut squash, Swiss chard, and minced garlic. Sauté until the vegetables are soft. This can take about 8 minutes. Add the bacon and stir.

3. Once you are ready to stuff the pork chops, you can make about 1-inch slits through the thickest parts. Stuff the pork with about 3 tablespoons of the filling. Season the pork with salt and pepper on both sides.

4. Heat up some oil in a cast iron skillet and pan fry the pork chops. About 3 minutes on each side. Remove from the pan and set aside.

5. Using the same skillet, sauté the onions until fragrant and translucent. Add the rest of the ingredients and allow to simmer until slightly thick. Place the pork chops back in the pan and simmer for 10 minutes or until the pork chops are cooked to your preference.

Nutritional Information

- Low-Fat, Low-Carb, High Protein

Prep Time:	4 hours
Cook Time:	30 minutes
Total Time:	4 hours and 30 minutes
Servings	4
Calories	225
Total Fat	5.7 grams
Saturated Fat	2 grams
Protein	24.1 grams
Cholesterol	70.2 mg
Carbohydrates	13.5 grams

Extra Tip:

- You can also serve this dish over some cheesy or plain grits, mashed potatoes, steamed rice or slices of toasted baguette.

Hasselback Potato Skillet Bake

What You Need:

- 6 to 8 pieces of baby Yukon Gold potatoes – just use enough to fill the size of your cast iron skillet.
- 8 tbsp. of melted unsalted butter
- 4 large garlic cloves, minced
- 4 tbsp. of finely minced herbs of your choice
- Salt and pepper, to taste
- 4 tbsp. of grated Parmesan cheese

Let's Make It:

1. Preheat your oven to 425 degrees F. make sure that you clean the potatoes properly. Scrub them to remove extra dirt on the skin.

2. Take one potato and slice a thin strip from the bottom. This will give you a flat base to keep the potato in place. Follow the same steps for the rest of the potatoes.

3. Slice the potatoes across – about 1/8 apart, but make sure that you do not cut the potatoes all the way through.

4. In a bowl, combine melted butter, garlic and herbs. Brush the mixture on top of the potatoes. Remember, do not soak the potatoes because we are keeping it light.

5. Bake for 1 hour – basting every 15 to 30 minutes. The potatoes will be crispy on the outside and really tender on the inside.

Nutritional Information

Prep Time:	20 minutes
Cook Time:	1 hour
Total Time:	1 hour of 20 minutes
Servings	6 to 8
Calories	144
Total Fat	3 grams
Saturated Fat	1 gram
Protein	2.9 grams
Cholesterol	31 mg
Carbohydrates	27 grams

Extra Tip:

- You can use any long, narrow and waxy heirloom potatoes if you cannot find any Yukon gold potatoes.

- For your herbs, you can use parsley, thyme and rosemary

- To keep you from slicing the potatoes all the way through, you can place a pair of chopsticks in on both sides to serve as your guide.

Seared Scallops with Sautéed Cucumbers

What You Need:

For the Cucumbers:

- 2 large English cucumbers, seeded and sliced into ¼ inch thick slices
- Pinch of pepper
- ½ tsp of salt
- 2 tbsps. of butter
- ¼ cup of low-fat sour cream
- 1 tsp of olive oil

For the scallops:

- 2 tsp. of olive oil
- 1 tsp of butter
- 1 tbsp. of chopped dill
- Salt and pepper to taste

- 1 and ¼ lbs. of dry sea scallops, cleaned.

Let's Make It:

1. Start by marinating the cucumber slices in salt. Let it sit for about 30 minutes to extract as much water. Squeeze, drain and set aside. (you can do this in advance)

2. Melt butter and add the oil to the cast iron skillet. Add the sliced cucumbers and season with pepper. Let it wilt a little before adding the sour cream. Once the cucumbers are done, about 5 minutes, remove from the pan and set it aside.

3. Melt the butter and add the oil to the same pan. Season the scallops with salt and pepper. Pan sear the scallops, about 2 to 3 minutes per side. Do not overcook otherwise the scallops will get really tough and rubbery.

4. Add the cooked cucumbers and gently mix everything together. serve warm.

Nutritional Information

- Low-Carb, Low-Calorie, High Protein, Low Fat

Prep Time:	25 minutes
Cook Time:	35 minutes
Total Time:	1 hour

Servings	4
Calories	204
Total Fat	9 grams
Saturated Fat	4 grams
Protein	19 grams
Cholesterol	48 mg
Carbohydrates	12 grams

Cast Iron Skillet Zucchini Lasagna

What You Need:

- 1/2 cup of button mushrooms, sliced
- 2 to 3 large cloves of garlic, minced
- 1/2 tbsp. of extra virgin olive oil
- 5-6 medium sized zucchinis, peeled and sliced into thin ribbons
- 1 (14.5 oz.) can of diced tomatoes
- 1 (8 oz.) can of tomato sauce
- 3 tbsps. of tomato paste
- 1 and 1/2 tsp. of dried oregano
- 1/2 tsp. of crushed red pepper flakes
- Salt and ground black pepper, to taste
- 2 and 1/2 Tbsp. of freshly chopped basil, divided

- 2 Tbsp. of chopped fresh parsley leaves
- 1 cup of part-skim mozzarella cheese, grated
- 2/3 cup of fat-free cottage cheese
- 1/3 cup of low-fat ricotta cheese for garnish, optional
- a sprinkle of parmesan cheese for garnish, optional

Let's Make It:

1. In a large cast iron skillet, heat up the oil and brown the garlic, and mushrooms. Season with salt and pepper. Sauté for about 3 minutes.
2. Add the diced tomatoes and cook it down for about 2 minutes. Add the herbs, tomato sauce and bring to a boil for about 5 minutes.
3. Add the zucchini noodles. And gently toss to avoid damaging the noodles. Cook for about 3 more minutes.
4. Remove from the heat and gently stir in the cheeses. Cover the pan and allow the residual heat to melt the cheese.
5. Sprinkle with parmesan and chopped basil.

Nutritional Information

- Lower in Carb, Gluten Free, Low Fat, Low Cholesterol, Vegetarian and Vegan-Friendly

Prep Time:	15 minutes
Cook Time:	20 minutes
Total Time:	35 minutes
Servings	4 to 6
Calories	271
Total Fat	7.9 grams
Saturated Fat	3 grams
Protein	12.7 grams
Cholesterol	15 mg
Carbohydrates	37.2 grams

Extra Tip:

- You can use your mandolin or your vegetable peeler to make those zucchini ribbons.

- You can also use spinach as an added source of iron and protein.

One Skillet Seafood Alfredo

What You Need:

- 1 and ½ cups uncooked mini penne pasta
- 2 tbsp. of extra virgin olive oil
- 2 tbsp. of minced garlic
- ¼ cup of minced onion
- 1 and ¾ cups of low sodium chicken broth
- 1 and ¾ cups of low fat or 2% skim milk
- 2 tbsp. of flour
- 1 (8 oz.) package of crab sticks, cut into small logs
- ½ lb. pack of peeled and cooked shrimps
- 1 cup of freshly grated parmesan cheese
- Salt and pepper, to taste
- 4 large basil leaves, chopped
- Fresh parsley, chopped

Let's Make It:

1. In a large cast iron skillet, heat the olive oil and sauté the onions and garlic for about 1 minute. Add the chicken broth, milk and whisk in the flour. Add the uncooked pasta, and bring to a gentle boil.

2. Simmer the dish for about 15 minutes, stirring constantly to keep the pasta from sticking. Once cooked, add the shrimps and the crab sticks and cook for another 3 minutes.

3. Turn the heat off and sprinkle Parmesan cheese on top. Season with salt and pepper.

Nutritional Information

- High Protein, Low Carb, Pescetarian

Prep Time:	5 minutes
Cook Time:	20 minutes
Total Time:	25 minutes
Servings	4 to 5
Calories	350
Total Fat	13 grams
Saturated Fat	4.1 grams
Protein	24.9 grams
Cholesterol	162.5 mg
Carbohydrates	30.6 grams

Extra Tip:

- You can use any smaller types of pasta such as bow-tie or macaroni.

Skinny Lemon Glazed Chicken Chops

What You Need:

- 4 pieces of chicken breast fillets (skinless) (about 4 oz. each)
- ¾ cup of Japanese Panko bread crumbs
- 2 large garlic cloves, minced
- ½ tsp salt
- ¼ tsp fresh ground pepper
- ¼ cup of freshly squeezed lemon juice
- ¼ cup of raw honey
- 1 to 2 tbsps. of Tabasco (or to taste)
- 1 tbsp. of extra-virgin olive oil
- Non-Stick Cooking spray

Let's Make It:

1. In a shallow bowl, combine the bread crumbs, garlic, salt, and pepper and mix well.

2. Dredge each piece of chicken breast on both sides. Ensure that they are evenly coated.

3. Spray your cast iron skillet with non-stick cooking spray and place over medium heat. Add the oil and wait until it is hot enough to fry in. Add the breaded chicken breasts and fry until golden brown. This process shall take around 6 minutes per side.

4. While the chicken breasts are frying, combine the honey, tabasco and lemon juice together and set aside.

5. Once the chicken chops are fried and completely cooked, remove them from the pan and then slowly heat up the honey and lemon mixture.

6. Allow to simmer for about 30 seconds. The sauce should be sticky and has a consistency of a slightly thick syrup.

7. Place the chicken pieces back in the pan and toss to coat.

Nutritional Information

- Paleo Friendly, High Protein, Low Fat, Low Carb

Prep Time:	12 minutes
Cook Time:	15 minutes

Total Time:	27 minutes
Servings	4
Calories	256
Total Fat	6 grams
Saturated Fat	1.5 grams
Protein	27 grams
Cholesterol	55 mg
Carbohydrates	26 grams

Easy Festive Seafood Paella

What You Need:

- 1 cup of long grain rice
- 1 and 1/2 cups of water
- ½ cup of white wine
- 2 tbsp. of extra virgin olive oil
- 2 large tomatoes, diced
- 1 medium onion, diced
- 1 pinch of saffron
- 3 large cloves of garlic, minced
- ¼ tsp of cayenne pepper
- 1 tsp of ground black pepper
- ½ lb. of salmon fillet
- ½ lb. of shrimp, deveined
- ½ lb. of scallops

- 1 (8 oz.) pack of frozen peas (thawed)

Let's Make It:

1. Heat your cast iron skillet and add the olive oil. Sauté the onions until soft and translucent, about 4 minutes. Add the minced garlic and the diced tomatoes. Cook down for 5 minutes.

2. Add the rice and toast the grains for a while. This will make sure that each grain is evenly coated with the aromatics.

3. Add the saffron and continue stirring the rice mixture for about 30 seconds or until well incorporated. Add the wine and allow to cook through. Next, add the water and stir well.

4. Season with salt, pepper, and cayenne pepper. Mix well. Cover so the rice could absorb the liquid and for each grain to cook well. This will take about 20 to 30 minutes.

5. Once the rice is almost cooked, arrange the seafood on top and drizzle with a little more olive oil and cover to cook. This will take around 10 to 20 minutes.

6. Serve with lemon slices.

Nutritional Information

Prep Time:	20 minutes
Cook Time:	60 minutes
Total Time:	1 hour and 20 minutes
Servings	6 to 8
Calories	309
Total Fat	5.8 grams
Saturated Fat	1.2 grams
Protein	27.5 grams
Cholesterol	110 mg
Carbohydrates	35 grams

Extra Tip:

- It is always good to use Paella rice. But if you do not have one, then you can always use long grain rice in its place.

One Skillet Holiday Mexican Quinoa

What You Need:

- 2 tbsp. of extra virgin olive oil
- 1 medium yellow onion, diced
- 2 large cloves garlic, minced
- 1 medium red bell pepper, diced
- 1 medium yellow bell pepper, diced
- 1 tsp of ground cumin
- 1 tsp of smoked paprika
- 1 tbsp. of chili powder
- 1 cup of uncooked quinoa, rinsed
- 1 small sweet potato, peeled and cut into ½" chunks
- 1 (14.5 oz.) can of diced tomatoes (No-Salt)
- 1 (10 oz.) can of diced tomatoes and chilies (mild)

- 1 (15 oz.) can of cooked black beans, rinsed and drained
- 1 and ½ cups of low sodium vegetable stock or water
- juice of 1 large lime
- ¼ cup of fresh chopped cilantro
- Extra:
    - Cilantro
    - lime wedges,
    - avocado, or
    - cheese for serving, optional

Let's Make It:

1. In your cast iron skillet, heat up the oil and sauté the onions and garlic. After 5 minutes, add the sweet potatoes, and cook until softened – about 4 minutes.
2. Add the bell peppers and the spices. Mix well and allow to cook some more.

3. Add the quinoa, the canned tomatoes, black beans, and your vegetable stock. Cover and allow to cook for 20 more minutes. When the quinoa has absorbed the stock, you are ready to squeeze in some lime and add the cilantro.

4. Serve with your choice of topping.

Nutritional Information

- Vegetarian, Vegan, High Protein, Low Fat, Low Cholesterol

Prep Time:	10 minutes
Cook Time:	30 minutes
Total Time:	40 minutes
Servings	6 to 8
Calories	207
Total Fat	5.9 grams
Saturated Fat	0.8 gram
Protein	12.8 grams
Cholesterol	0 mg
Carbohydrates	54 grams

Extra Tip:

- You can also add frozen corn kernels and sliced jalapeno peppers when making this dish.

Catalan Sauté of Chicken with Sausage, Capers and Herbs

What You Need:

- 1 and ½ lbs. of whole chicken (legs, thigh and drumstick separated) – skins removed, excess fat trimmed
- ¾ tsp of fine kosher salt, divided
- ¼ tsp of freshly ground pepper, plus more to taste
- 2 tbsps. of canola oil, divided
- 1 (8 oz.) pack of sweet Italian turkey sausage links, sliced into rounds
- 2 tbsps. of low-fat butter
- 2 large ripe tomatoes, diced
- 2 large cloves of garlic, crushed
- 1 large shallot, finely minced
- ½ cup of white wine
- ½ cup salt-free or low-salt chicken broth

- 1 and ½ tsp. of cornstarch
- 2 tbsps. of capers, rinsed
- 1 tsp. of freshly grated lemon zest

Bouquet Garni: - make this by tying the sprigs together using a kitchen twine.

- 1 sprig fresh rosemary
- 1 sprig fresh thyme
- 2 tbsps. of finely chopped flat-leaf parsley, for garnish

Let's Make It:

1. Season the chicken pieces with ¼ tsp salt and ¼ tsp of pepper. Set aside.

2. Heat your cast iron skillet and start browning the sausages in 1 tsp of oil. Once cooked, remove from the pan and drain on a piece of paper towel. Set aside.

3. Add the rest of the oil and melt the butter over medium to high heat. Add the pieces of chicken and brown each piece on all sides. This will take

around 5 minutes per side per chicken. Remove from the skillet and transfer onto a plate. Set aside

4. Place the skillet back on the heat and sauté the tomatoes, shallots, the rest of the salt and pepper. Cook until all the liquid from the tomatoes has evaporated. Around 7 to 8 minutes.

5. Add the wine and your bouquet garni. Simmer for another 3 minutes. Place the chicken pieces back in the skillet and then add the sausages. Gently stir and coat the chicken with the sauce and cover. Allow to slowly cook for about 20 to 25 minutes.

6. In a small bowl, combine the broth and the cornstarch and mix well. Set aside.

7. Remove the bouquet garni and place the chicken and sausages on a serving platter.

8. Using the same skillet, make the sauce by mixing the cooking liquid with the cornstarch and broth mixture, capers, and lemon zest. Mix well and allow to thicken. Serve the chicken with the sauce and chopped parsley.

Nutritional Information

- Gluten Free, Low Carb, Low Calorie, High Protein

Prep Time:	20 minutes

Cook Time:	1 hour and 5 minutes
Total Time:	1 hour and 25 minutes
Servings	6
Calories	198
Total Fat	9 grams
Saturated Fat	3 grams
Protein	19 grams
Cholesterol	89 mg
Carbohydrates	5 grams

Steak with Glazed Carrots and Turnips

What You Need:

- 2 tbsp. of extra-virgin olive oil, divided
- 1 tbsp. of organic butter
- 1 pound of turnips, sliced into thick matchsticks (about 3 medium-sized)
- 1 lb. pack of small carrots - sliced lengthwise – each carrot should be about 5-inch long
- ¾ tsp of salt and pepper, divided
- 1 lb. sirloin or top round steak, about an inch thick – trimmed and cleaned – sliced in half (crosswise)
- 1 tsp of minced fresh rosemary or about ½ tsp. dried
- 1 tbsp. of red-wine vinegar
- 2 tbsps. of packed brown sugar

Let's Make It:

1. Preheat your oven to 450 degrees F.

2. Season the steaks with rosemary and half of the salt and pepper. Set aside.

3. Heat your cast iron skillet and add 1 tbsp. of oil and butter and sauté the carrots and turnips. Season with half of the salt and pepper. Cook until softened, about 10 minutes and remove from the pan.

4. Heat the remaining oil over medium to high flame. Sear the marinated steaks until brown. About 2 minutes per side. Remove from the heat and set aside.

5. Place the vegetables back in the skillet and add the brown sugar and mix well. Push the veggies to the sides of the skillet and add the steak in the middle. Roast in the oven for about 10 minutes or until the steaks have reached their desired doneness.

6. Drizzle vegetables with vinegar before serving.

Nutritional Information

- Gluten free, Low Calorie, Egg Free, High Protein, Low Carb

Prep Time:	10 minutes
Cook Time:	30 minutes
Total Time:	40 minutes
Servings	4
Calories	328
Total Fat	15 grams
Saturated Fat	5 grams
Protein	24 grams
Cholesterol	67 mg
Carbohydrates	25 grams

"Healthy eating is not a diet. It is called eating healthy."

Chapter Three: 10 Healthy Holiday Dessert Recipes

Who is ready for dessert? I know that even if we are too busy or too lazy or in a serious diet, we will always have room for some quick, delicious and healthy desserts. These recipes will surely satisfy your sweet tooth cravings in no time.

In this chapter, I will help you:

- Learn new ways to use your cast iron skillet such as using it to make tasty and healthy desserts.
- Find out how to spice up your desserts with some tips and suggestions.

Cast Your Skillet Fears Aside and Make Room for Some Healthy Desserts

Here are 10 amazingly easy, healthy and delicious dessert recipes that you can make using your cast iron skillet.

Bananas Foster Upside-Down Cake

What You Need:

- 1/2 cup of softened butter, divided
- 2 tbsps. of rum
- 1 cup of firmly packed light brown sugar
- 1/2 cup of chopped pecans, toasted
- 2 medium-size ripe bananas, sliced into half-moons
- 7 pieces of maraschino cherries, halved
- ¾ cup of granulated sugar, divided
- 2 large organic eggs, separated
- ¾ cup of milk
- ½ cup of sour cream
- 1 tsp of vanilla extract
- 2 cups of all-purpose baking mix

- ¼ tsp of ground cinnamon

Let's Make It:

1. Place your cast iron skillet over medium heat and start melting half of the butter. Add the rum and the brown sugar over the butter. stir slightly and remove from the heat.

2. Sprinkle the chopped pecans over the butter and sugar mixture. Gently press the sliced bananas on top of the pecans. Arrange it neatly and add the sliced cherries, cut-side down. Set aside.

3. Preheat your oven to 350 degrees F.

4. In a mixing bowl, cream the butter and ½ cup of granulated sugar. Add the egg yolks, milk, sour cream and vanilla extract. Blend the cake mix and the powdered cinnamon. Set aside.

5. In another bowl, beat the egg whites until you form soft peaks. Gently whisk in the remaining sugar. Fold the mixture in with the batter and transfer into your cast iron skillet. Spread evenly.

6. Bake for 45 to 50 minutes or until a cake tester inserted in the middle comes out clean.

Nutritional Information

- High Fiber, Low Cholesterol, Low Calorie, Vegetarian

Prep Time:	20 minutes
Cook Time:	53 minutes
Total Time:	1 hour and 13 minutes
Servings	10
Calories	295
Total Fat	7.5 grams
Saturated Fat	2 grams
Protein	4.2 grams
Cholesterol	0.2
Carbohydrates	54.2 grams

Extra Tip:

- You can omit the rum if you are serving cake for the kids.

Low Carb Gooey Skillet Brownie for Two

What You Need:

- 5 tbsp. of almond flour
- 3 tbsp. of cocoa powder
- 1 tsp of baking powder
- 3 tbsp. of your choice of sweetener
- 3 tbsp. of water
- 2 tbsp. of avocado oil
- 1 large organic egg
- ¼ tsp. of pure vanilla extract
- 1 tbsp. of sugar-free chocolate chips (optional)

Let's Make It

1. Preheat your oven to 325 degrees and grease a small cast iron skillet with a little non-stick cooking spray.

2. Whisk all the ingredients together (in a bowl) until creamy and smooth. Pour the batter into your skillet and spread evenly.

3. Bake for 13 to 16 minutes or until the top has puffed up but the middle still needs to be set. Serve warm.

Nutritional Information

- Low Carb, Low Calorie

Prep Time:	10 minutes
Cook Time:	16 minutes
Total Time:	26 minutes
Servings	2
Calories	198
Total Fat	23.81 grams
Saturated Fat	4.57 grams
Protein	7.14 grams
Cholesterol	214 mg
Carbohydrates	0 grams

Extra Tip:

- You can use melted butter instead of avocado oil if you cannot find one.

- You can serve this with low-carb ice cream.

Almond Butter Quinoa Brownies

What You Need:

- ¼ cup of softened unsalted butter
- ¾ cup of smooth or crunchy natural almond butter
- 2 large organic eggs
- ¾ cup of packed light brown sugar
- 1 tsp of pure vanilla extract
- ¾ cup of quinoa flour
- 1 tsp baking powder
- ¼ tsp salt
- 1 cup of semi-sweet chocolate

Let's Make It:

1. Preheat your oven to 350 degrees F. grease your skillet with non-stick cooking spray.
2. In a bowl, beat the butter and almond butter together until creamy. Add the eggs one at a time. Add the sugar and vanilla. Add the flour, baking

powder, and salt. Fold in the chocolate chips and transfer into your prepared cast iron skillet.

3. Bake for 25 to 30 minutes

Nutritional Information

- Low Carb, Low Fat, Low Calorie, Low Cholesterol

Prep Time:	15 minutes
Cook Time:	30 minutes
Total Time:	45 minutes
Servings	24
Calories	147
Total Fat	9 grams
Saturated Fat	3 grams
Protein	3 grams
Cholesterol	21 mg
Carbohydrates	15 grams

Extra Tip:

It can be challenging to find quinoa flour, so you can sub it with almond flour or you can make your own using a high powered blender or food processor.

Browned Butter Chocolate Chip Skillet Cookie

What You Need:

- ½ cup of softened butter
- 1 large organic egg
- 1 tsp of pure vanilla extract
- 2 tbsp. of coconut sugar
- ¼ cup of natural granulated sweetener
- 2 cups of fine almond flour
- ½ tsp of sea salt
- ½ cup of sugar-free chocolate chips (optional)

Let's Make It:

1. Preheat your oven to 350 degrees F. and melt the butter in your 9 in cast iron skillet over medium to high heat. Once the butter starts to bubble, cover the pan to keep the butter from splitting. Cook until the butter turns brown but not burnt. The entire process can take about 5 minutes. Allow to cool.

2. In a bowl, whisk the egg and vanilla together. slowly add the sugar and granulated sweetener. Add the rest of the ingredients and gently fold in the chocolate chips.

3. Add the cooled melted butter and blend well.

4. Transfer the batter to the skillet and spread evenly. Bake for 25 to 30 minutes or until a toothpick comes out clean when inserted in the center.

Nutritional Information

- Low Carb, Vegetarian, Vegan-Friendly

Prep Time:	15 minutes
Cook Time:	30 minutes
Total Time:	45 minutes
Servings	10 to 12
Calories	231
Total Fat	15.7 grams
Saturated Fat	6 grams
Protein	5 grams
Cholesterol	28 mg
Carbohydrates	5 grams

Extra Tip:

- Make this vegan by replacing the egg with flax egg.

Ultra-Lite Peach Cobbler

What You Need:

For the Filling:

- 2 (14.5-oz.) cans of sugar-free peaches
- ¼ tsp. of cinnamon
- A pinch of nutmeg
- ½ tsp. glucomannan powder
- 1 packet stevia or Splenda
- 2 tbsp. of unsalted butter (plus 1 tbsp. more to grease the baking dish)

For the Crust:

- 1 cup plus 2 tbsp. of Carbalose flour
- 6 tbsp. of resistant wheat starch
- ½ cup plus 1 tbsp. of shortening or butter
- ¼ tsp. of fine salt
- ¼ cup ice cold water

Let's Make It:

1. Make the crust by blending the flour, wheat starch and salt together. Slowly mix in the butter and water until it forms a smooth dough. Wrap in plastic sheet and place in the fridge to chill and set.

2. Grease the bottom of your skillet with 1 tbsp. of butter. set aside.

3. Preheat your oven 350 degrees F.

4. In a large bowl, combine the cinnamon, nutmeg, stevia, and peaches. Mix until well combined and transfer to your prepared skillet.

5. Dollop bits of butter all around the peach mixture. Set aside.

6. Roll out your dough and flatten it to about ½ inch thick. Cover your cobbler with the dough and crimp the edges to seal. You can use any leftover dough to decorate your cobbler.

7. Bake for 25 minutes. Serve warm.

Nutritional Information

- Low Carb, Low Sugar

Prep Time:	30 minutes

Cook Time:	25 minutes
Total Time:	55 minutes
Servings	6
Calories	330
Total Fat	26.3 grams
Saturated Fat	13.7 grams
Protein	1.23 grams
Cholesterol	70 mg
Carbohydrates	8.1 grams (net)

Extra Tip:

- You can use xanthan gum instead of glucomannan powder.
- Carbalose flour is a non-carbo loaded version of wheat flour. If you are not into the low carb diet, you can use regular wheat flour or white flour.
- To replace resistant wheat starch, you can use vital wheat gluten, oat fiber or wheat protein.

Flourless Brownies

What You Need:

- 2 oz. of unsweetened chocolate squares
- 1 cup of unsalted butter
- 1 and ½ cups of Splenda
- 4 large organic eggs
- 4 large egg yolks
- 1 tbsp. of vanilla
- 6 tbsp. of cocoa powder

Let's Make It:

1. Preheat your oven to 350 degrees F. Grease your skillet with non-stick baking spray.
2. Heat a small pot of water and place a heat proof bowl over it. Place the chocolate squares and butter in the bowl and melt them together. Cool for at least 10 minutes.

3. In a blender, whisk together the eggs and Splenda. Drizzle the melted chocolate and add the cocoa powder.

4. Spread in your large skillet and bake for 50 minutes. Cool completely before slicing.

Nutritional Information

Prep Time:	20 minutes
Cook Time:	50 minutes
Total Time:	1 hour and 10 minutes
Servings	48
Calories	84
Total Fat	9 grams
Saturated Fat	2 grams
Protein	2 grams
Cholesterol	44 mg
Carbohydrates	3 grams

One Pan Pumpkin Bars

What You Need:

- 8 tbsp. of softened butter
- 1/2 cup each:
    - Brown sugar
    - White sugar
- 1 large organic egg
- 1 tsp of pure vanilla extract
- ¾ cup of pumpkin puree
- 1/2 tsp each of:
    - baking soda
    - Salt
    - ground cinnamon
- 1 and ½ cups of all-purpose flour
- 1 cup of bittersweet chocolate chips

- 1/3 cup of chopped pecans

Let's Make It:

1. Preheat your oven to 350 degrees F. grease your cast iron skillet with non-stick baking spray. Set aside.

2. In a bowl, blend the butter, sugars, egg and vanilla extract together until creamy. Fold in the pumpkin puree.

3. In another bowl, sift together flour, salt, baking soda, and cinnamon. Mix in with the pumpkin mixture.

4. Fold chocolate chips and pecans.

5. Transfer into your prepared skillet and bake for 20 to 25 minutes.

Nutritional Information

- Low Carb, Low Cholesterol, Low Calorie

Prep Time:	10 minutes
Cook Time:	20 to 25 minutes
Total Time:	35 minutes
Servings	16 to 20
Calories	148
Total Fat	9 grams

Saturated Fat	3 grams
Protein	2 grams
Cholesterol	0 mg
Carbohydrates	17 grams

Extra Tip:

- Serve this with light cream cheese frosting or your butterscotch syrup. Ice cream is also a great partner for this.

Easy Holiday Cherry Cobbler

What You Need:

Cherry Filling:

- 2 (14.5 oz.) cans of pitted red cherries
- 2 tbsp. of honey
- 1/2 tsp of xanthan gum
- 2 tbsp. of lemon juice

Topping:

- 1 cup of almond flour
- 1 tsp of baking powder
- 2 tbsp. of stevia or sweetener of choice
- 2 tbsp. of melted coconut oil
- 2 large organic eggs

Let's Make It:

1. Preheat your oven to 425 degrees F.

2. Mix the ingredients for the cherry filling (in q bowl). Transfer in a greased 9 inch cast iron skillet. Set aside.

3. Combine the ingredients for the toppings. Your mixture should be soft but not runny. Spoon dollops of the toppings on top of the cherry filling.

4. Bake for 15 minutes or until the crust is golden brown in color.

Nutritional Information

- Low Carb, Low Calorie, Vegetarian

Prep Time:	20 minutes
Cook Time:	15 minutes
Total Time:	35 minutes
Servings	10
Calories	147
Total Fat	9 grams
Saturated Fat	2 grams
Protein	4 grams
Cholesterol	2 mg
Carbohydrates	13 grams

Apple Zucchini Crisps

What You Need:

- 1/4 cup of lightly packed brown sugar
- 2 tsp of cinnamon, divided
- a pinch of nutmeg
- 3 tbsp. of fresh lemon juice
- 1 cup of apples, peeled and thinly sliced
- 2 cups of zucchini, peeled, halved and thinly sliced
- 1/3 cup of almond meal (not flour)
- 1/3 cup of sliced almonds
- 1/3 cup of chopped pecans
- 1 tsp of pure vanilla extract
- 1/4 cup melted butter

Let's Make It:

1. Preheat your oven to 375 degrees F.

2. In a bowl, combine the apples, lemon juice and zucchini and place in you 8 inch cast iron skillet. Spread evenly.

3. In a small bowl, combine sugar, 1 tsp of cinnamon, nutmeg, almond meal, almonds and pecans. Add the melted butter and vanilla and toss together. crumble the mixture evenly over the apples and zucchinis.

4. Bake for 30 minutes.

Nutritional Information

- Low carb, Low Calorie, Zero Trans Fat

Prep Time:	15 minutes
Cook Time:	30 minutes
Total Time:	45 minutes
Servings	9
Calories	156
Total Fat	12 grams
Saturated Fat	3.8 grams
Protein	2.5 grams
Cholesterol	42 mg
Carbohydrates	10 grams

Airy Almond Skillet Cookie

What You Need:

- Egg whites from 3 large eggs
- 1/8 tsp of salt
- 1 tsp pure vanilla extract
- 1 cup of sugar
- ½ cup of whole almonds – roasted and chopped finely

Let's Make It:

1. Grease your skillet with non-stick cooking spray and set aside. preheat your oven to 250 degrees F.
2. Beat egg whites in an electric mixer until fluffy. Gradually add the sugar and salt. Continue beating until the mixture forms stiff peaks. Do not overbeat because the egg whites will dry out.
3. Fold in the almonds gently. You want to keep the air in.
4. Transfer into your greased skillet and bake for 30 to 45 minutes or until the tops have browned.

Nutritional Information

- Low calorie, Low Carb, Low Fat

Prep Time:	10 minutes
Cook Time:	45 minutes
Total Time:	50 minutes
Servings	20 to 25 spoonfuls
Calories	16
Total Fat	0.2 gram
Saturated Fat	0 gram
Protein	0.4 gram
Cholesterol	0 mg
Carbohydrates	3.7 grams

Extra Tip:

- You can replace almonds with pistachios or walnuts as well. Cashews will work too.

Healthy Chocolate Cake

What You Need:

- 1 (15 oz.) can of unseasoned cooked black beans
- 6 large organic eggs
- 1/2 tsp of sea salt
- 1 tbsp. of pure vanilla extract
- 5 and ½ tbsp. melted coconut oil
- 1/2 cup + 2 tbsp. of organic honey
- 2 tsp. of baking powder
- 6 tbsp. of unsweetened cocoa powder

Let's Make It:

1. Preheat your oven to 350 degrees F. Grease your 9-12 inch cast iron skillet with baking spray and dust the bottom of the pan with a little bit of cocoa powder. Set aside.

2. In a blender or food processor, combine all the ingredients together until well incorporated.

3. Transfer to your prepared skillet and bake for 35 minutes or until a toothpick inserted in the middle comes out clean. Allow to completely cool before serving with your choice of fruits, powdered sugar or frosting.

Nutritional Information

- Low calorie, low carb, vegetarian

Prep Time:	10 minutes
Cook Time:	35 minutes
Total Time:	45 minutes
Servings	6 to 8
Calories	182
Total Fat	13 grams
Saturated Fat	4.6 grams
Protein	8 grams
Cholesterol	156 mg
Carbohydrates	10 grams

"Keep my skillet good and greasy."

Chapter Four: Best Practices for Cast Iron Cooking

I have been a huge fan the cast iron pan for many years. But my love affair with this kitchen wonder didn't start smoothly. Honestly, I didn't have any idea on how to properly use it – more so cook with it and care for it. But through years of practice and advice from fellow home cooks, I was able to get as much best practices as I can to improve my cast iron pan cooking skills.

In this chapter, I will help you:

- Find out why it is great to cook with cast iron pans.

- Learn how to properly cook with your cast iron pan or skillet.

Why I Love My Cast Iron Pan

There are so many reasons why I consider my cast iron pans my trusted kitchen "*BFFs.*" Here are some that you will also come to discover when you start using yours.

It’s a multipurpose cookware.

Forget about using a lot of different pots and pans. Your cast iron skillet is not for frying your favorite Southern-fried chicken. You can also make stews, fried rice, paella and even bake cakes and cookies in it. This will help you not just save time on washing up, but will also help you save money on buying cookware.

A well-seasoned cast iron pan is naturally non-stick

You do not need to cook with so much grease especially if you are trying to watch what you eat. You can sauté without the added oil or even bake without greasing the pan too much.

So easy to clean.

Forget about using warm soapy water to clean up your pan. Because with some water and a little wipe, you can easily clean your cast iron skillet. Remember that too much scrubbing and using soap will remove the “seasoning” or flavor from your pan.

Sturdy and will last long.

Do you know that your cast iron pan, if used well, can even outlive you and the next generations after you? It saves you money and it makes a great heirloom piece.

Beneficial to your health.

Cooking with a cast iron pan or skillet can definitely be a great way for you to boost your iron intake. It keeps your immune system strong!

Top Cast Iron Cooking Tips

If you want to make sure that you will be able to make the most out of your cast-iron pan, here are some tips that you may want to take note of and practice.

- **Season your Cast Iron Pan** – the pan's "seasoning" or patina builds up as you use it. The pan collects the flavors that make all your food cooked in it well seasoned and properly cooked. It also eliminates the roughness and creates a more non-stick cooking surface for your food.

- **Never Use Soap** – this will remove the seasoning! So clean it up with water, dry it up and coat with your choice of oil. I often use canola.

- **Use high heat to sear your meat-** do not be scared to use as much heat as you want. It won't crack, nor will it damage the coating.

- **Do not overcrowd the pan when frying** – this is probably the tip that you should keep in mind most because it can guarantee your safety. Since cast iron pans can keep a consistently high temperature, overcrowding the pan can cause the oil to spill over – which can cause fire and can cause serious burns.

"A home-cooked meal is a labor of love."

Conclusion

Together we can make better, healthier and more beautiful food without the fuss and hassles of washing too many pots and pans. Using your cast iron skillet or your choice of the pan, you can use the recipes we have provided to help create a festive yet nutritious spread not just for the holidays, but for any day of the week that you wish to make home cooked meals for you and your family.

We hope that the recipes and the contents of this book have inspired you to spend more time in the kitchen, as much as we are.

Bonus: Your FREE Gift

As a token of our appreciation, please take advantage of the **FREE Gift** - a lifetime **VIP Membership** at our book club.

Follow the link below to download your FREE books:

http://bit.ly/vipbookclub

As a VIP member, you will get an instant **FREE** access to exclusive new releases and bestselling books.

19163047R00060

Printed in Great Britain
by Amazon